IT'S A BANJO CHRISTMAS

Favorite Christmas Songs
Arranged for Bluegrass Banjo
by Bob Cox   Compiled by Ron Middlebrook

Calligraphy by George Ports

Santa Barbara

CONTENTS

FORWARD

THE POPULARITY OF THE FIVE-STRING BANJO HAS GROWN IMMENSELY IN THE PAST FEW YEARS. THE FIVE-STRING HAS A SOUND EVERYONE ENJOYS AND ITS BLUEGRASS PICKING WILL BRING MELODIES OF JOY TO US ALL.

THIS NEW BOOK OF THE FIVE-STRING BRINGS US SONGS OF CHRISTMAS ARRANGED FOR US IN THAT GOOD OLE' BLUEGRASS STYLE. MOST OF THE SONGS TAKE YOU THROUGH A BEGINNING, AND INTERMEDIATE ARRANGEMENTS PLUS WE PUT IN A COUPLE OF ADVANCED ARRANGEMENTS TOO.

HERE YOU CAN SEE HOW A TUNE IS TAKEN FROM A SIMPLE MELODY TO AN ADVANCED BANJO PICKING MELODY. WE HOPE THAT THIS BOOK WILL NOT ONLY HELP YOU LEARN MANY NEW TUNES BUT ITS SYSTEMATIC APPROACH WILL LEAD YOU INTO ARRANGING YOUR OWN TUNES BY STARTING WITH THE BASIC MELODY AND WORKING FROM THERE TO A GREAT SOUNDING BANJO SOLO.

THE BANJO IS GREAT FUN, WE ALL KNOW THAT, SO LET'S GET PICKIN'.

BANJO BOB COX

CHRISTMAS WITHOUT MUSIC?

Christmas has many contrasts. It is a time of feasts and fasts; of joyful revelry and solemn ritual; of happy family reunions for some, and a special kind of loneliness for others; it is a time of holly, ivy, fir trees, and mistletoe — all handed down from ancient, forgotten cults — and also a time of tinsel, spun glass, glittery baubles and paper angels. Great air-conditioned cathedrals form the backdrop for scenes of medieval pageantry to the sound of thousand-year-old chants, while all around the world, simple village churches and wayside chapels are gathering places for those who wish to pray and sing together by candlelight.

Christmas without music can scarcely be imagined; the sounds of Christmas can be merry, from "Jingle Bells" to Tschaikowsky's "Nutcracker Ballet"; or they can be as solemn and impressive as Handel's "Messiah" or a children's choir singing "Silent Night". From the first days of December, carols and bells resound in every town — from the shops as well as from loudspeakers strung on street poles. Not so very many years ago it was common, especially in the German communities of the midwest, for little bands of musicians to roam the streets, stopping here and there to play rousing old-country Christmas songs and dances. People stopped on the street to listen, to drop their pennies in the kettle, and perhaps to sing along. It took stamina to stand on a cold, windy street corner and play "Joy To The World" on a trumpet. The music is still very much with us, literally permeating the air around us from morning 'til night. Perhaps that is why there still are hardy and persistent people who gather together on Christmas Eve, all mufflered, mittened, and ear-muffed, to stroll through their communities and sing all their favorite carols. If the weather is really too unbearable, there is always the parsonage or someone's home in which to congregate, with the assurance of "refreshments" — no doubt including eggnog or punch, or some other harmless version of the potent Wassail Bowl.

The custom of caroling began in medieval England when groups of strolling musicians played in the streets or before the homes of important personages on holidays and other special occasions. They were paid by the town and were supplied with dashing uniforms. Originally, they were town watchmen, called "waits," who announced the hours of the night with high-pitched tones from an instrument called a "shawm". The shawm is thought to have been introduced from the Near East in about the 12th century, and is the ancestor of our present-day oboe. Eventually the instrument itself became known as a "wait", as did the tunes that were played by the various musical guilds, such as the London Waits, or the Coventry Waits. Today, the word in a musical context simply means "a street performer of Christmas music."

The word "carol" is thought to be derived from the medieval French word "carole", meaning "a round dance," in which the dancers formed a close circle. They were the popular songs and dances of the time — the folk music — as opposed to the music of the church. There were carols for every holiday or special occasion: May Day, Easter, the beginning of Lent, the end of Lent, harvest festivals, all the saints' days, not to mention the celebrations associated with the coming of spring, summer, autumn, and winter. However, today the word "carol" is almost exclusively applied to those songs that are sung only at Christmas time.

Carols as we know them are a product of the 15th century, when religious songs appeared that were written in the common, everyday language, instead of in Latin, and familiar folktunes replaced the prescribed forms of church music. The stories of the Bible lent themselves naturally to such songs, especially the dramatic events surrounding the Nativity. Certain non-religious carols were inspired by popular Christmas customs such as "going-a-wassailing", and the ceremonious serving of the boar's head at the Christmas feast. The earliest printed carol that has survived to the present time is the "Boar's Head Carol", which is still sung every year at Queen's College, Oxford. It appeared in a collection that was issued in 1521. Unfortunately, the other carols in the collection have been lost. Other early carols are "O Sanctissima; The Wassail Song; God Rest Ye Merry, Gentlemen; Deck The Halls With Boughs of Holly"; and "I Saw Three Ships". This last-named carol sounds very much like "Here We Go 'Round The Mulberry Bush", which children have been singing for centuries, and the tune is familiar in every part of the world where there are English-speaking people. There are many lovely old carols dating back to the 15th and 16th centuries that are not familiar to American ears, but are still sung in England, Ireland, Scotland, and Wales, where they originated. In addition, of course, every European country has its own tradition of original Christmas music, much of which was brought to this country by our grandparents or their grandparents.

The 16th century saw the rise of Protestantism and the beginning of the struggles of the early 17th century which culminated in the Thirty Years' War. At the end of this war, in 1648, the political power of the Pope was broken, and at last the Church and State were separate. In the meantime, the teachings of Calvin had spread, and some of his followers, called "Puritans" because of their excessive zeal in trying to eradicate any traces of "popishness' in the church, had become numerous. The Puritans were repressed, if not actually persecuted, and this harassment eventually led, in 1620, to the most determined of them fleeing to the New World. In England, in 1647, the Puritan Parliament under Oliver Cornwell abolished almost all amusements and holidays, including Christmas, and strict Puritan rules of conduct were imposed upon the people. Christmas was just another day. After the restoration of the monarchy in 1660, there was a revival of Christmas celebrations in England, but there was not the same interest in carols and caroling, except in parts of Ireland and Wales, and among small groups in England who had managed to remember the songs and keep them alive. It was not until the 19th century that interested musicians, historians, and publishers began to collect and preserve the old carols (and add some new ones). The practice of carol singing all but vanished, and it is largely due to the efforts of a few dedicated persons that more than 500 English carols and other folktunes, some traced back to the 15th century, have been preserved.

In America, Christmas was outlawed by the Puritans, who thoroughly disapproved of the extravagance, feasting, dancing and general frivolity of the celebration, and were even more vociferous in their denunciation of all the heathen aspects of the holiday such as the use of evergreens and ritual fires. They ignored the day in their church services, and in 1659 forbade by law any Christmas observances in their settlements. The law was repealed in 1681, but it was nearly 150 years before there was any widespread celebration of Christmas in the New England area.

The early American settlers were not all Puritans, however, and Christmas was kept alive by the Dutch, Germans, and the British royalists. As America grew and immigration increased, new settlers from all parts of Europe brought with them their customs, legends, folklore, native foods, treasured family recipes, music, dances, and unique ways of celebrating their many varied and ancient holidays. Today, an "American" Christmas has an unimaginable number of regional variations and a great wealth of music from all parts of the world, but the traditional carols are known and loved by everyone.

BANJO FINGERBOARD CHART
G TUNING

SHARPS # MOVE UP 1 FRET   FLATS b MOVE BACK 1 FRET

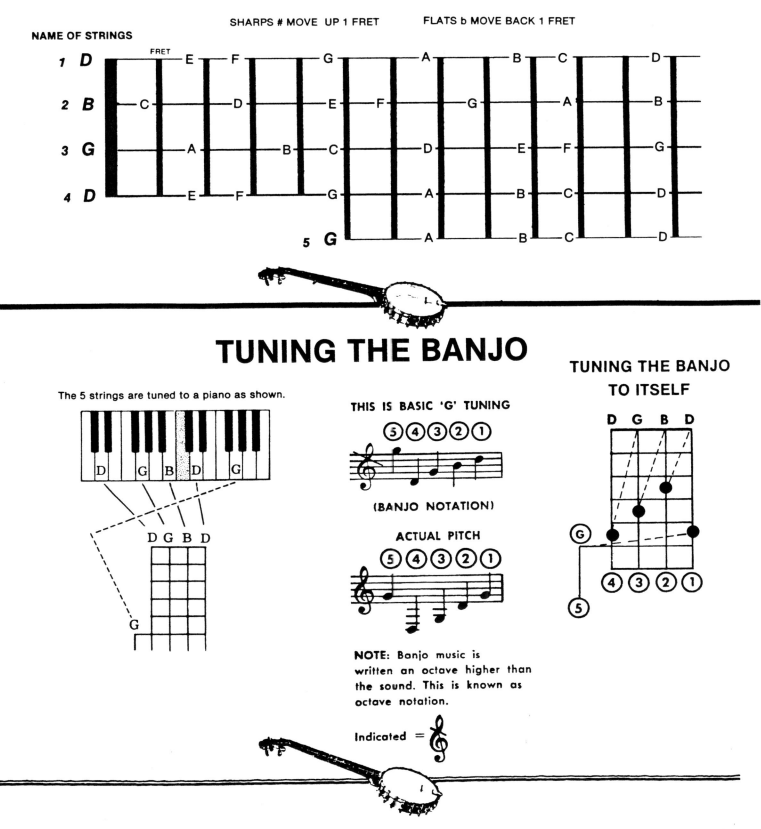

TUNING THE BANJO

The 5 strings are tuned to a piano as shown.

THIS IS BASIC 'G' TUNING

(BANJO NOTATION)

ACTUAL PITCH

NOTE: Banjo music is written an octave higher than the sound. This is known as octave notation.

Indicated =

TUNING THE BANJO TO ITSELF

TABLATURE

All of the music in this book will be written in tablature. In tab. There are 5 lines, each representing a string on the banjo. Numbers are placed in the lines corresponding to the frets on which you place your fingers.

FIRST POSITION CHORDS

MAJOR CHORDS

The symbol o above a string means it is to be sounded open.

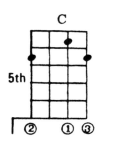
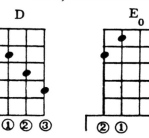
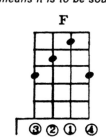
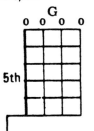

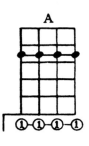

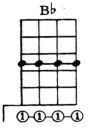
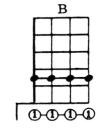
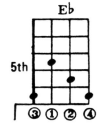
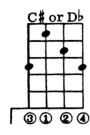
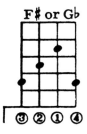

7th CHORDS

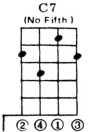
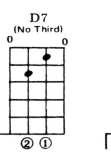
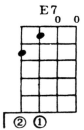
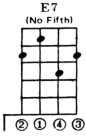
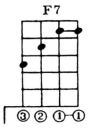

In this fingering the fifth string would provide the fifth of the chord.

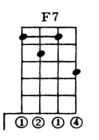
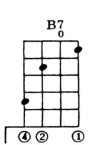

MINOR CHORDS

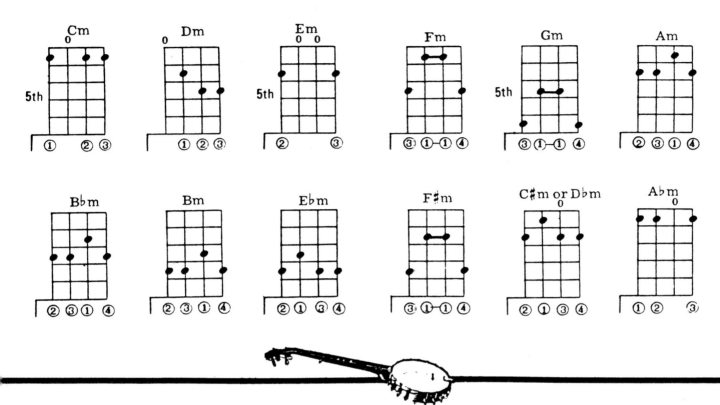

Cm   Dm   Em   Fm   Gm   Am

B♭m   Bm   E♭m   F♯m   C♯m or D♭m   A♭m

MINOR 7 CHORDS

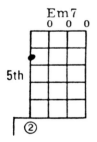

Em7

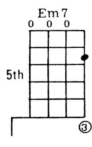

Em7

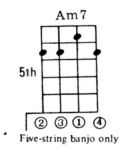

Am7

Five-string banjo only

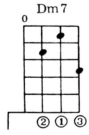

Dm7

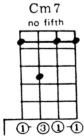

Cm7
no fifth

The fifth string would
provide the fifth of the
chord.

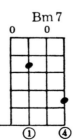

Bm7

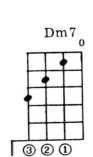

Dm7

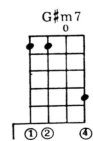

G♯m7

Words To The Songs Contained
In This Book

Away in a Manger

Away in a manger, no crib for His bed,
The little Lord Jesus laid down His sweet head.
The stars in the sky looked down where He lay,
The little Lord Jesus, asleep on the hay.

The cattle are lowing, the poor Baby wakes,
But little Lord Jesus, no crying He makes.
I love Thee, Lord Jesus, look down from the sky,
And stay by my cradle till morning is nigh.

Be near me, Lord Jesus, I ask Thee to stay
Close by me forever and love me, I pray!
Bless all the dear children in Thy tender care,
And Take us to heaven, to live with Thee there.

Go Tell It On The Mountain

While shepherds kept their watching
O'er silent flocks by night
Behold throughout the heavens,
There shone a holy light:

Go, tell it on the mountain,
Over the hills and ev'rywhere;
Go, tell it on the mountain
That Jesus Christ is born.

The shepherds feared and trembled
When lo! above the earth
Rang out the angel chorus
That hailed Our Saviour's birth:

Down in a lowly manger
Our humble Christ was born
And God sent us salvation,
That blessed Christmas morn:

When I was a seeker,
I sought both night and day;
I sought the Lord to help me,
And He showed me the way:

He made me a watchman
Upon the city wall,
And if I am a Christian,
I am the least of all.

Deck the Halls

Deck the halls with boughs of holly,
Fa la la la la, la la la la;
'Tis the season to be jolly,
Fa la la la la, la la la la.
Don we now our gay apparel,
Fa la la, la la la, la la la;
Troll the ancient Yuletide carol,
Fa la la la la la la la la la.

See the blazing yule before us,
Fa la la la la, la la la la;
Strike the harp and join the chorus,
Fa la la la la, la la la la.
Follow me in merry measure,
Fa la la, la la la, la la la;
While I tell of Yuletide treasure,
Fa la la la la, la la la la.

Fast away the old year passes,
Fa la la la la, la la la la;
Hail the New Year, lads and lasses,
Fa la la la la, la la la la.
Sing we joyous, all together,
Fa la la, la la la, la la la;
Heedless of the wind and weather,
Fa la la la la, la la la la.

Hear the Glad Tidings

Hear the glad tidings,
Hear the glad tidings!
Now in Bethl'hem manger.
Born of the virgin,
Born of the virgin
Is the Christ, our Savior.

Angels are singing,
Kings gifts are bringing,
Shepherds are praying,
Cattle are kneeling
To the little Jesus,
To the Son of Mary
Who this day is born to us!

No room for Mary,
No room for Mary,
Full the inn with trav'lers;
So to a stable,
So to a stable
Did she go for shelter.

While Joseph watches,
While Joseph watches,
Safely Christ is sleeping.
See Mary smiling,
See Mary smiling
As she rocks the King.

Kneel we before Him,
Kneel we before Him,
Hear our glad song ringing:
"Glory to Jesus,
Glory to Jesus,
Glory everlasting!"

I Saw Three Ships

I saw three ships come sailing in,
On Christmas Day, on Christmas Day,
I saw three ships come sailing in,
On Christmas Day in the morning.

And what was in those ships all three?
On Christmas Day, etc.
And what was in etc.
On Christmas day in etc.

Our Saviour, Christ, and His Lady.

Pray, whither sailed those ships all three?

O, they sailed to Bethlehem.

And all the bells on earth shall ring.

And all the angels in heaven shall sing.

And all the souls on earth shall sing.

Then let us all rejoice and sing.

Jingle Bells

Dashing through the snow
In a one-horse open sleigh,
O're the fields we go,
Laughing all the way;
Bells on Bobtail ring,
Making spirits bright,
What fun it is to ride and sing
A sleighing song tonight!

Jingle bells, jingle bells!
Jingle all the way!
Oh what fun it is to ride
In a one-horse open sleigh!

A day or two ago,
I thought I'd take a ride,
And soon Miss Fanny Bright
Was seated by by side;
The horse was lean and lank;
Misfortune seemed his lot;
He got into a drifted bank,
And we, we got upsot.

A day or two ago,
The story I must tell
I went out on the snow
And on my back I fell;
A gent was riding by
In a one-horse open sleigh,
He laughed as there I sprawling lie,
But quickly drove away.

Now the ground is white
Go it while you're young
Take the girls tonight
And sing this sleighing song;
Just get a bobtailed bay
Two-forty as his speed
Hitch him to an open sleigh
And crack! you'll take the lead.

Jolly Old St. Nick

Jolly old Saint Nicholas, lean your ear this way!
Don't you tell a single soul what I'm going to say.
Christmas Eve is coming soon;now, you dear old man,
Whisper what you'll bring to me; tell me if you can.

When the clock is striking twelve, when I'm fast asleep,
Down the chimney broad and black, with your pack you'll creep.
All the stockings you will fing hanging in a row;
Mine will be the shortest one, you'll be sure to know.

Johnny wants a pair of skates; Susy wants a dolly;
Nellie wants a story book; she things dolls are folly.
As for me, my little brain isn't very bright;
Choose for me, old Santa Claus, what you think is right.

O Christmas Tree

O Christmas Tree, O Christmas Tree,
How stead fast are your branches!
Your boughs are green in summer's clime
And through the snows of wintertime.
O Christmas Tree, O Christmas Tree,
How stead fast are your branches!

O Christmas Tree, O Christmas Tree,
What happiness befalls me
When oft at joyous Christmastime
Your form inspires my song and rhyme.
O Christmas Tree, O Christmas Tree,
What happiness befalls me.

O Christmas Tree, O Christmas Tree,
Your boughs can teach a lesson
That constant faith and hope sublime
Lend strength and comfort through all time.
O Christmas Tree, O Christmas Tree,
Your boughs can teach a lesson.

O Come All Ye Faithful

O come, all ye faithful, joyful and triumphant,
O come ye, O come ye to Bethlehem!
Come and behold Him, born the King of Angels;

O come, let us adore Him;
O come, let us adore Him;
O come, let us adore Him,
Christ the Lord.

Sing, choirs of angels, sing in exultation,
O sing, all ye citizens of heaven above!
Glory to God in the highest:

Yea, Lord, we greet Thee, born this happy morning,
Jesus, to Thee be all glory giv'n;
Word of the Father now in flesh appearing:

Silent Night

Silent night, holy night!
All is calm, all is bright
Round yon Virgin Mother and Child.
Holy Infant, so tender and mild,
Sleep in heavenly peace!
Sleep in heavenly peace!

Silent night, holy night!
Shepherds quake at the sight.
Glories stream form heaven afar,
Heav'nly hosts sing "Alleluia!"
Christ the Saviour is born!
Christ the Saviour is born!

Silent night, holy night!
Wondrous star, lend thy light!
With the angels let us sing
Alleluia to our King!
Christ the Saviour is here,
Jesus the Saviour is here!

Silent night, holy night!
Son of God, love's pure light,
Radiant beams from Thy holy face,
With the dawn of redeeming grace,
Jesus, Lord, at Thy birth,
Jesus, Lord, at Thy birth!

THE SEVEN JOYS OF MARY

THE FIRST GOOD JOY THAT MARY HAD, IT WAS THE JOY OF ONE,
TO SEE THE BLESSED JESUS CHRIST WHEN HE WAS FIRST HER SON.
WHEN HE WAS FIRST HER SON, GOOD LORD, AND HAPPY MAY WE BE.
PRAISE FATHER, SON AND HOLY GHOST TO ALL ETERNITY!

THE NEXT GOOD JOY THAT MARY HAD, IT WAS THE JOY OF TWO,
TO SEE HER OWN SON, JESUS CHRIST MAKE THE LAME TO GO.
MAKE THE LAME TO GO, GOOD LORD, AND HAPPY MAY WE BE.
PRAISE FATHER, SON AND HOLY GHOST TO ALL ETERNITY!

THE NEXT GOOD JOY THAT MARY HAD, IT WAS THE JOY OF THREE,
TO SEE HER OWN SON, JESUS CHRIST MAKE THE BLIND TO SEE.
MAKE THE BLIND TO SEE, GOOD LORD, AND HAPPY MAY WE BE.
PRAISE FATHER, SON AND HOLY GHOST TO ALL ETERNITY!

THE NEXT GOOD JOY THAT MARY HAD, IT WAS THE JOY OF FOUR,
TO SEE HER OWN SON, JESUS CHRIST READ THE BIBLE O'ER.
READ THE BIBLE O'ER, GOOD LORD, AND HAPPY MAY WE BE.
PRAISE FATHER, SON AND HOLY GHOST TO ALL ETERNITY!

THE NEXT GOOD JOY THAT MARY HAD WAS THE JOY OF FIVE,
TO SEE HER OWN SON, JESUS CHRIST RAISE THE DEAD TO LIFE.
RAISE THE DEAD TO LIFE, GOOD LORD AND HAPPY MAY WE BE.
PRAISE FATHER, SON AND HOLY GHOST TO ALL ETERNITY!

THE NEXT GOOD JOY THAT MARY HAD, WAS THE JOY OF SIX,
TO SEE HER OWN SON, JESUS CHRIST UP ON THE CRUCIFIX.
UP ON THE CRUCIFIX GOOD LORD, AND HAPPY MAY WE BE.
PRAISE FATHER, SON AND HOLY GHOST TO ALL ETERNITY!

THE NEXT GOOD JOY THAT MARY HAD, IT WAS THE JOY OF SEVEN,
TO SEE HER OWN SON, JESUS CHRIST ASCENDING INTO HEAVEN.
ASCENDING INTO HEAVEN, GOOD LORD, AND HAPPY MAY WE BE.
PRAISE FATHER, SON AND HOLY GHOST TO ALL ETERNITY!

WHAT CHILD IS THIS?

WHAT CHILD IS THIS, WHO, LAID TO REST,
ON MARY'S LAP IS SLEEPING?
WHOM ANGELS GREET WITH ANTHEMS SWEET,
WHILE SHEPHERDS WATCH ARE KEEPING?

THIS, THIS IS CHRIST THE KING,
WHOM SHEPHERDS GUARD AND ANGELS SING:
HASTE, HASTE TO BRING HIM LAUD,
THE BABE, THE SON OF MARY.

WHY LIES HE IN SUCH MEAN ESTATE
WHERE OX AND ASS ARE FEEDING?
GOOD CHRISTIAN, FEAR: FOR SINNERS HERE
THE SILENT WORD IS PLEADING.

SO BRING HIM INCENSE, GOLD, AND MYRRH,
COME, PEASANT, KING TO OWN HIM;
THE KING OF KINGS SALVATION BRINGS,
LET LOVING HEARTS ENTHRONE HIM:

THE CHERRY TREE CAROL

WHEN JOSEPH WAS AN OLD MAN,
AN OLD MAN WAS HE,
HE MARRIED VIRGIN MARY,
THE QUEEN OF GALLILEE.

THEN MARY SPOKE TO JOSEPH SO MEEK
AND SO MILD,
"JOSEPH, GATHER ME SOME CHERRIES,
FOR I AM WITH CHILD."

THEN JOSEPH GREW IN ANGER, IN ANGER
GREW HE:
"LET THE FATHER OF THY BABY GATHER
CHERRIES FOR THEE."

THEN JESUS SPOKE A FEW WORDS, A FEW
WORDS SPOKE TO HE:
"LET MY MOTHER HAVE SOME CHERRIES,
BOW LOW DOWN, CHERRY TREE!"

THE CHERRY TREE BOWED DOWN, BOWED
LOW DOWN TO THE GROUND,
AND MARY GATHERED CHERRIES WHILE
JOSEPH STOOD AROUND.

WE WISH YOU A MERRY CHRISTMAS

WE WISH YOU A MERRY CHRISTMAS,
WE WISH YOU A MERRY CHRISTMAS,
WE WISH YOU A MERRY CHRISTMAS
AND A HAPPY NEW YEAR!

GLAD TIDINGS WE BRING
TO YOUAND YOUR KIN;
GLAD TIDINGS FOR CHRISTMAS
AND A HAPPY NEW YEAR!

PLEASE BRING US SOME FIGGY PUDDING
PLEASE BRING US SOME FIGGY PUDDING,
PLEASE BRING US SOME FIGGY PUDDING,
PLEASE BRING IT RIGHT HERE!

WE WON'T GO UNTIL WE GET SOME,
WE WON'T GO UNTIL WE GET SOME,
WE WON'T GO UNTIL WE GET SOME,
PLEASE BRIGHT IT RIGHT HERE!

WE WISH YOU A MERRY CHRISTMAS,
WE WISH YOU A MERRY CHRISTMAS
WE WISH YOU A MERRY CHRISTMAS
AND A HAPPY NEW YEAR!

13

AWAY IN A MANGER

Away In A Manger

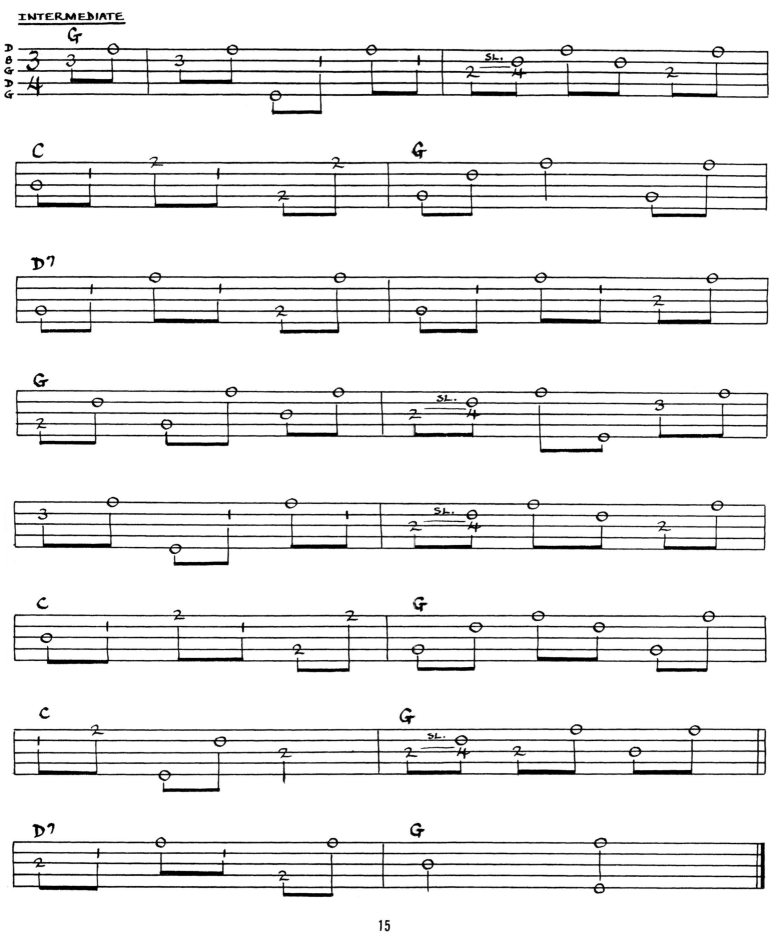

DECK THE HALLS

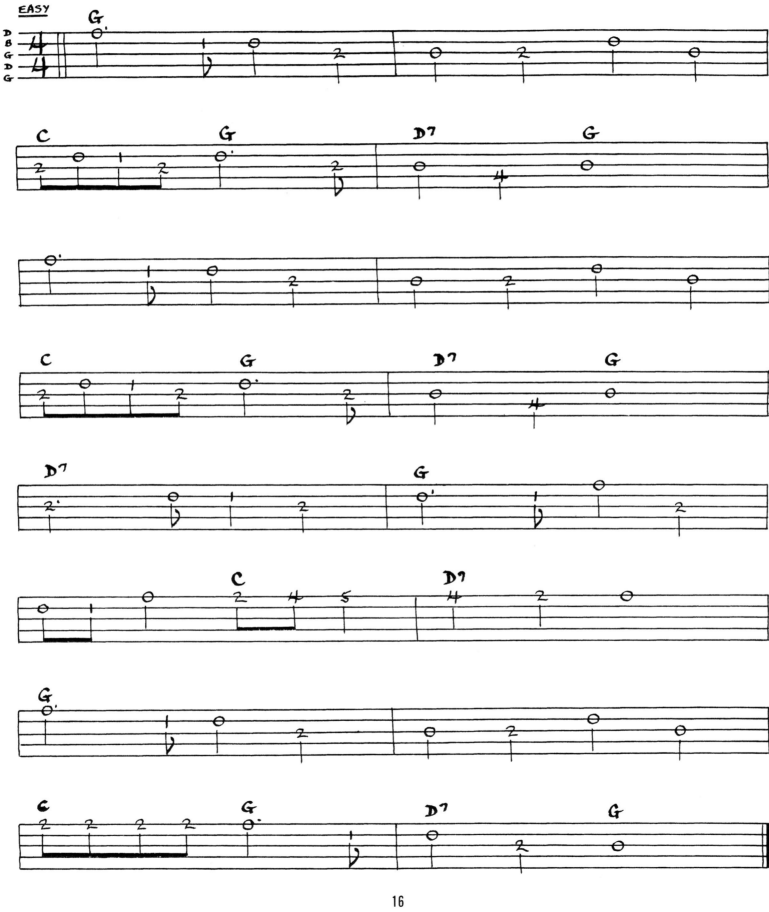

DECK THE HALLS

Go Tell It On The Mountain

Go Tell It On The Mountain

Hear The Glad Tidings

I Saw Three Ships

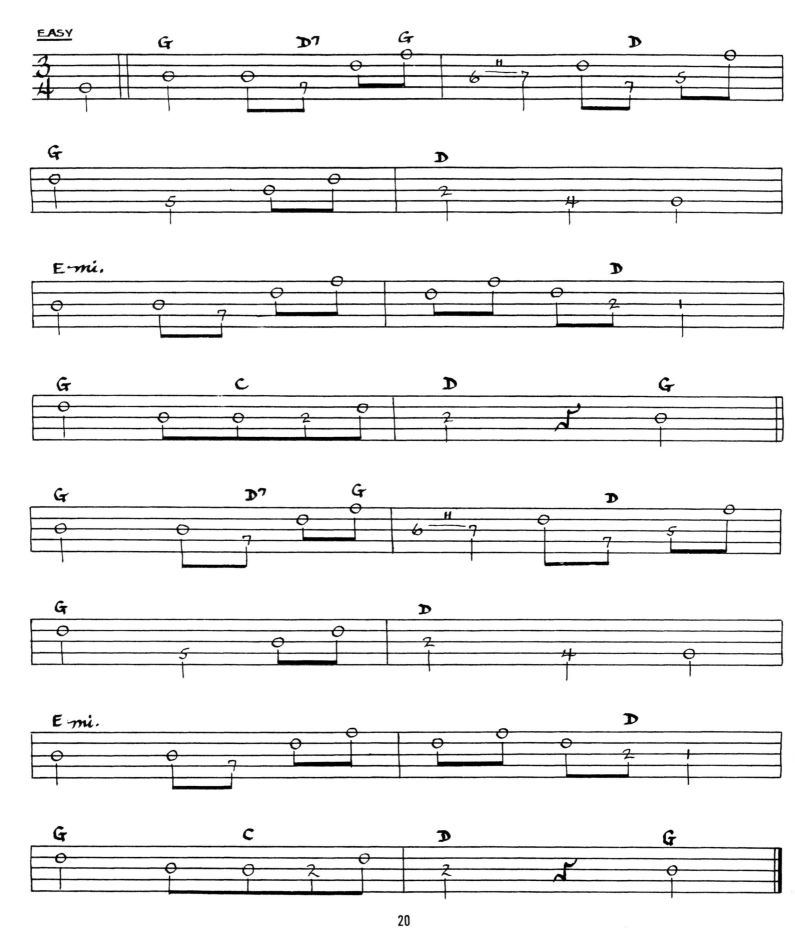

20

Jingle Bells

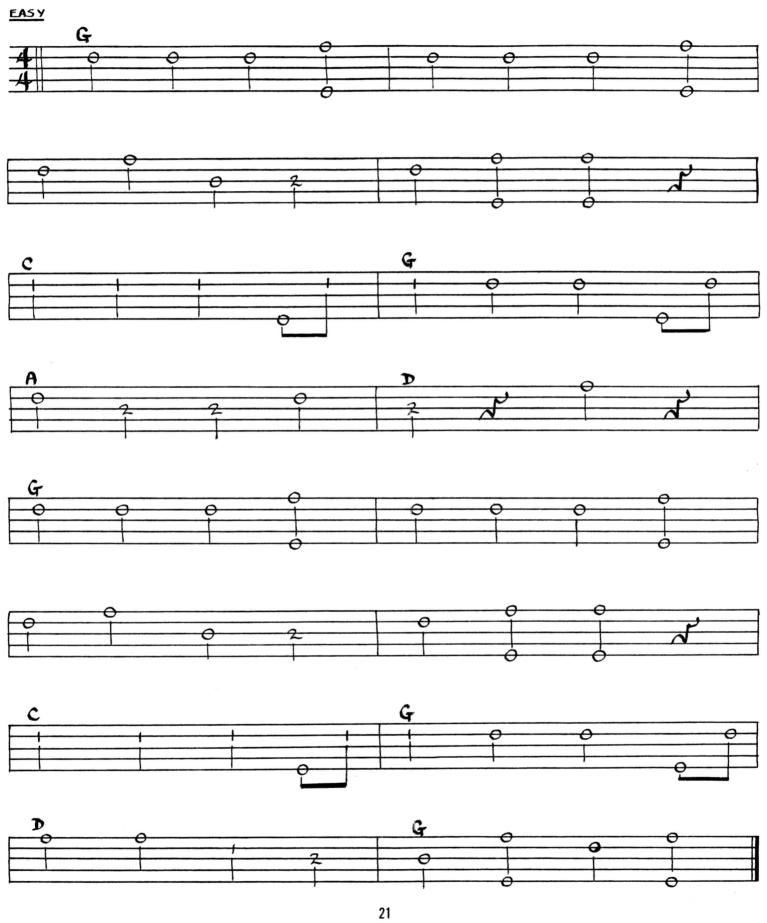

Jingle Bells

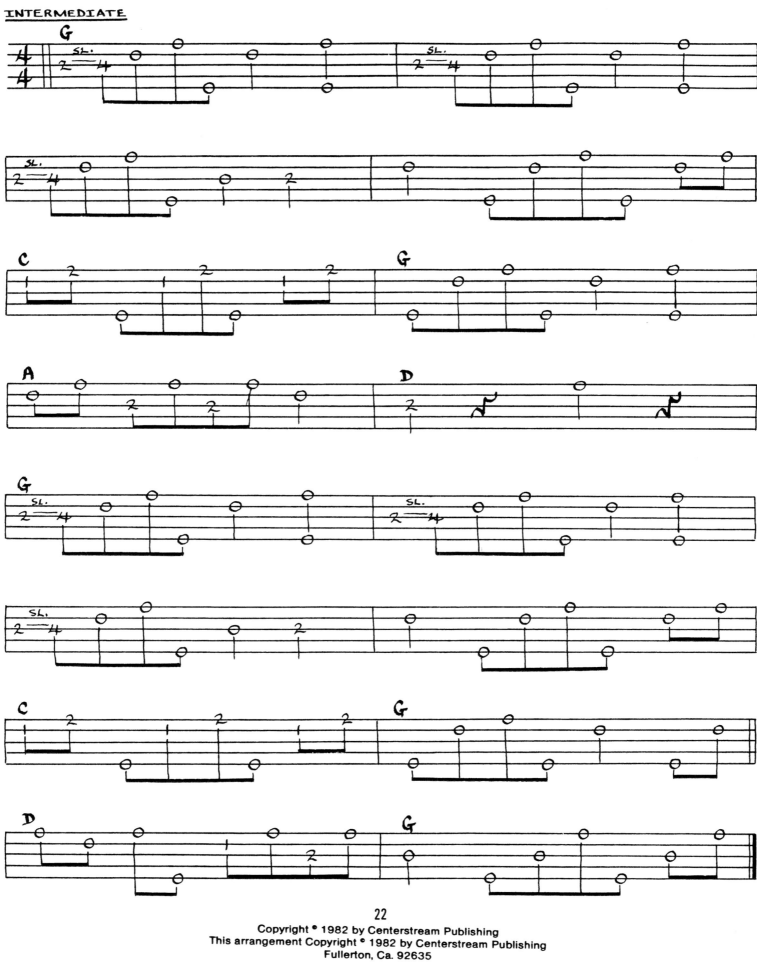

Jingle Bells

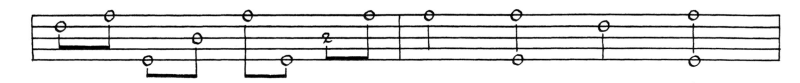

JOLLY OLD ST. NICK

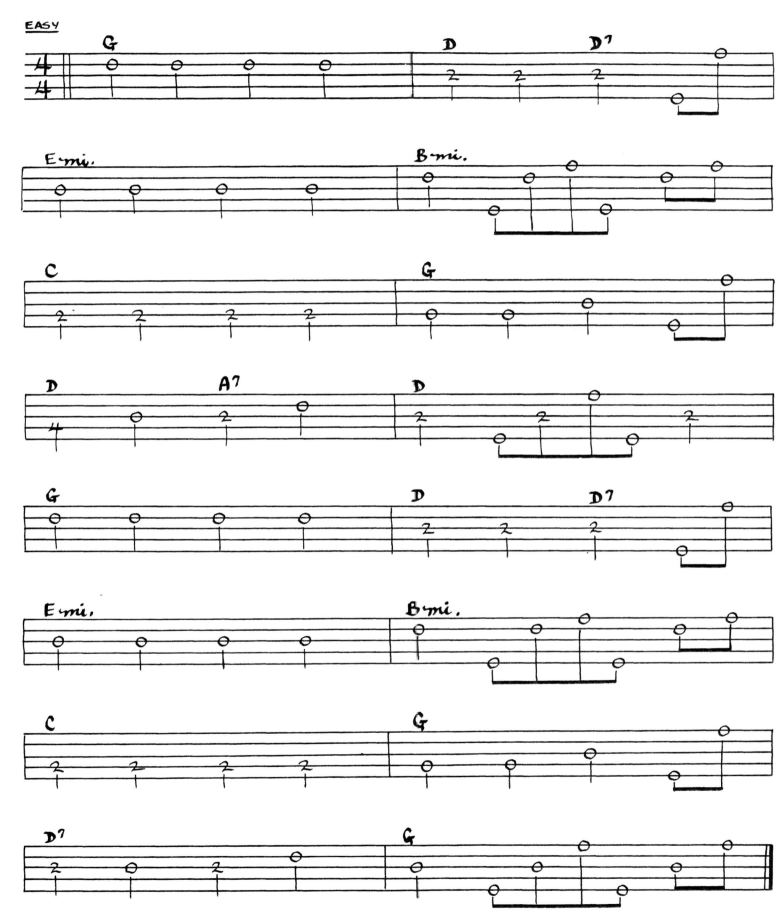

JOLLY OLD ST. NICK

INTERMEDIATE

O Christmas Tree

27

O Christmas Tree

O Come All Ye Faithful

O Come All Ye Faithful

REINDEER HORNPIPE

by Bob Cox

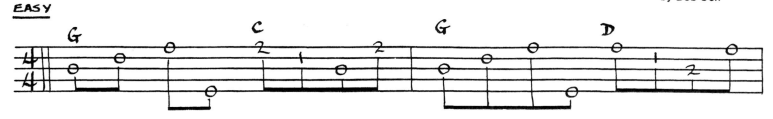

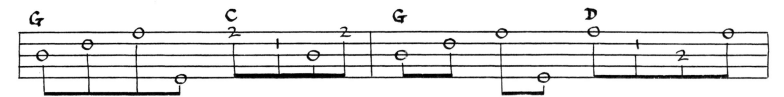

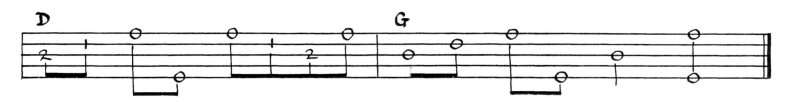

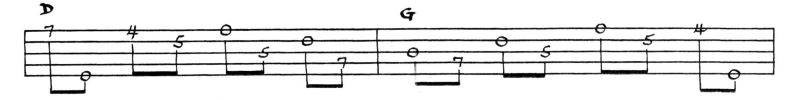

REINDEER HORNPIPE

INTERMEDIATE

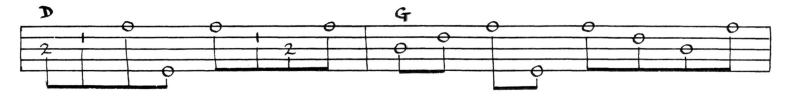

PICKIN' ON A CHRISTMAS EVE

by Bob Cox

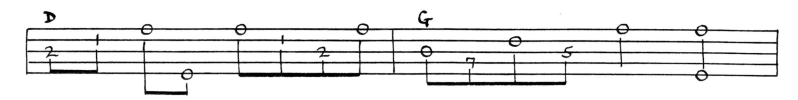

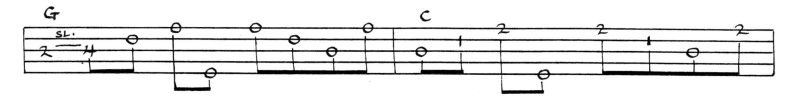

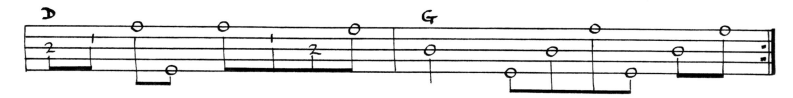

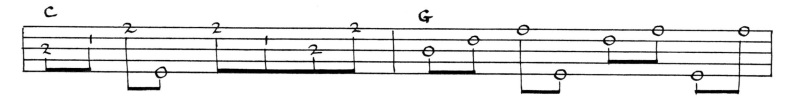

32

Pickin' On A Christmas Eve

INTERMEDIATE

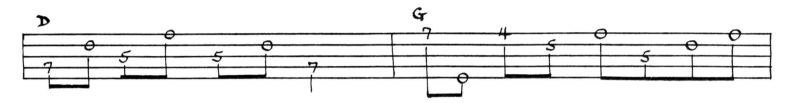

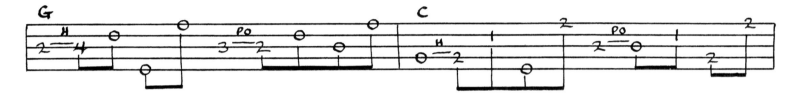

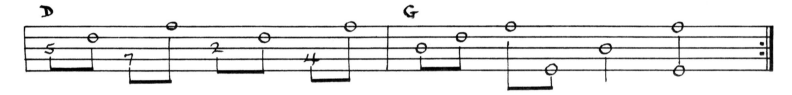

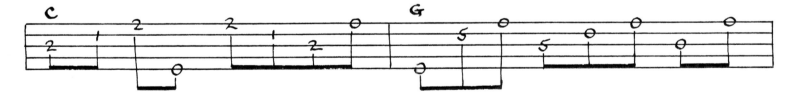

33

Santa Claus Had A Breakdown

by Bob Cox

INTERMEDIATE

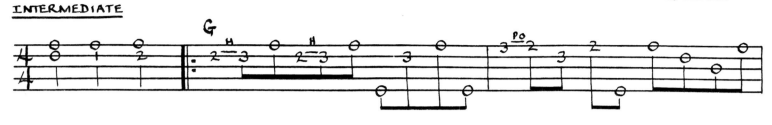

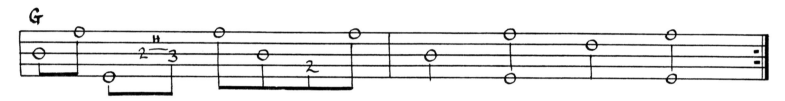

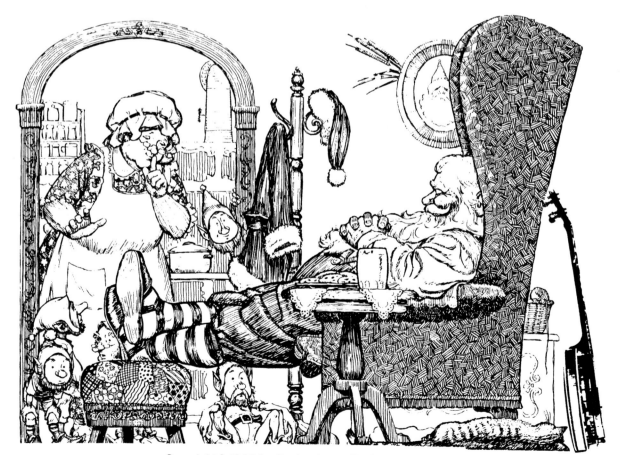

Silent Night

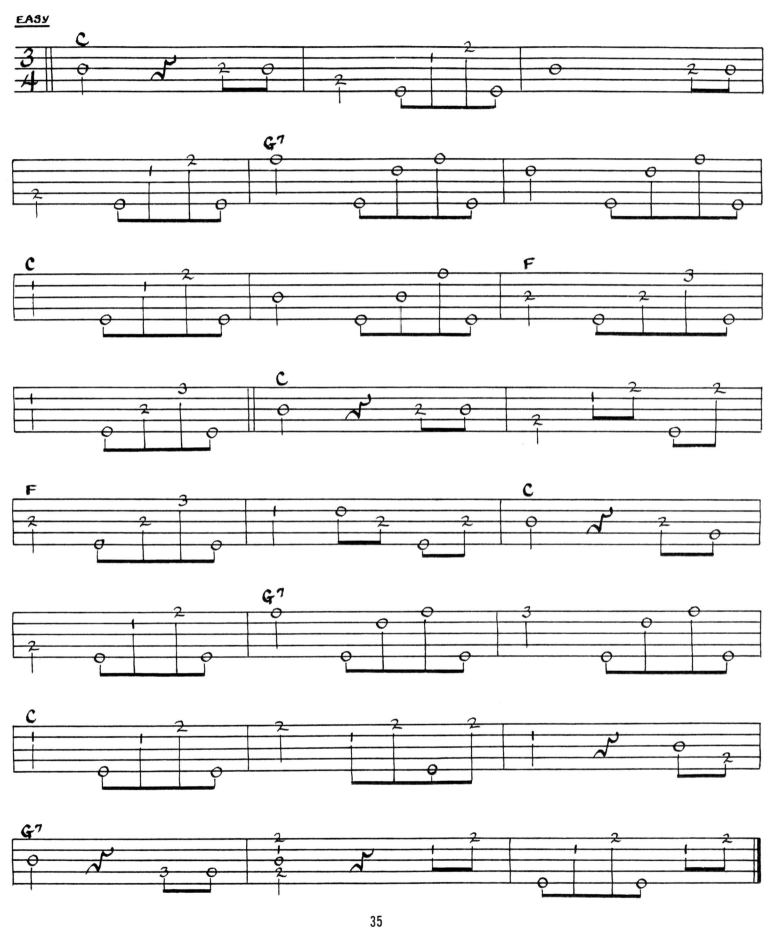

Silent Night

The Cherry Tree Carol

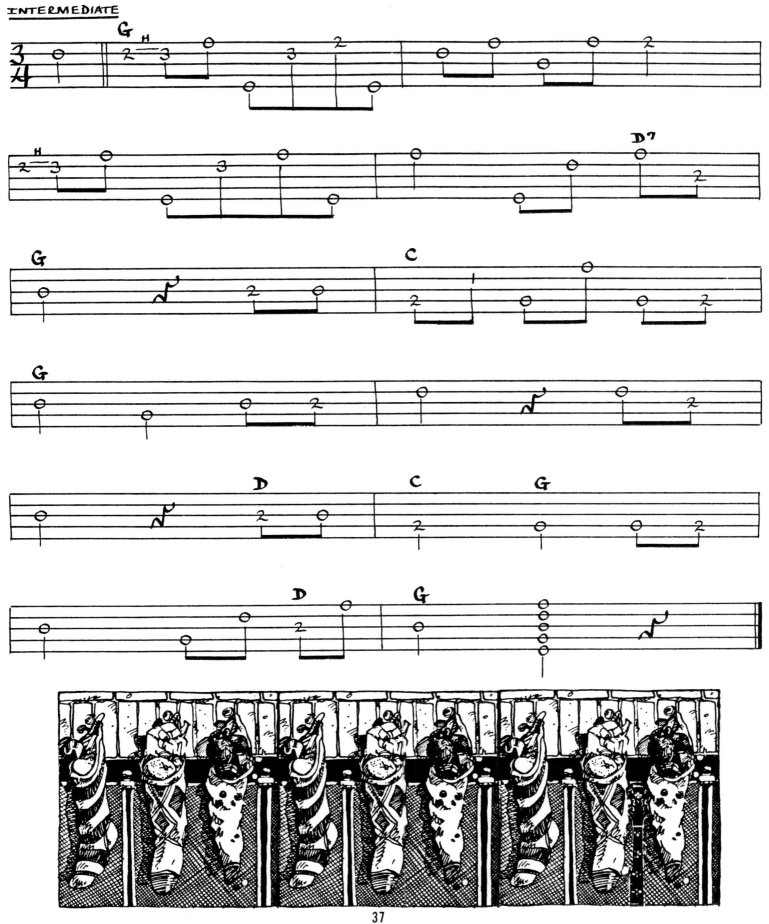

Copyright © 1982 by Centerstream Publishing
This arrangement Copyright © 1982 by Centerstream Publishing
Fullerton, Ca. 92635

The Seven Joys Of Mary

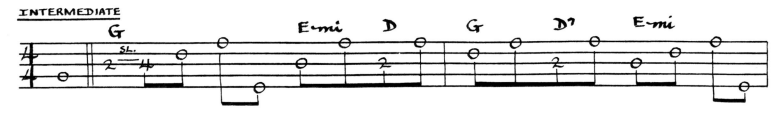

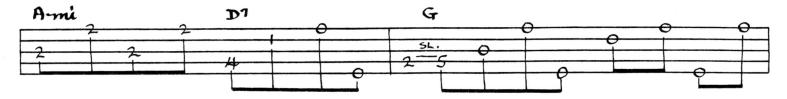

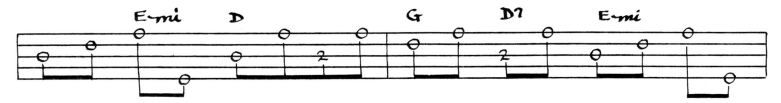

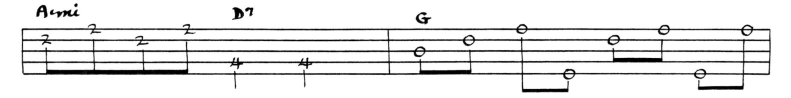

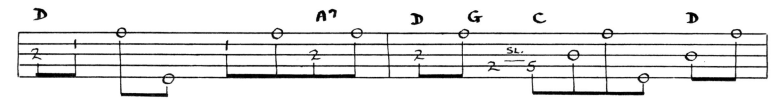

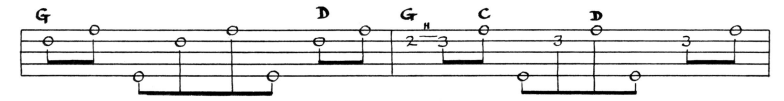

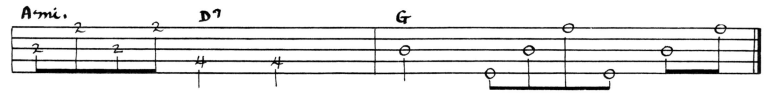

38

We Wish You A Merry Christmas

WHAT CHILD IS THIS?
(GREENSLEEVES)

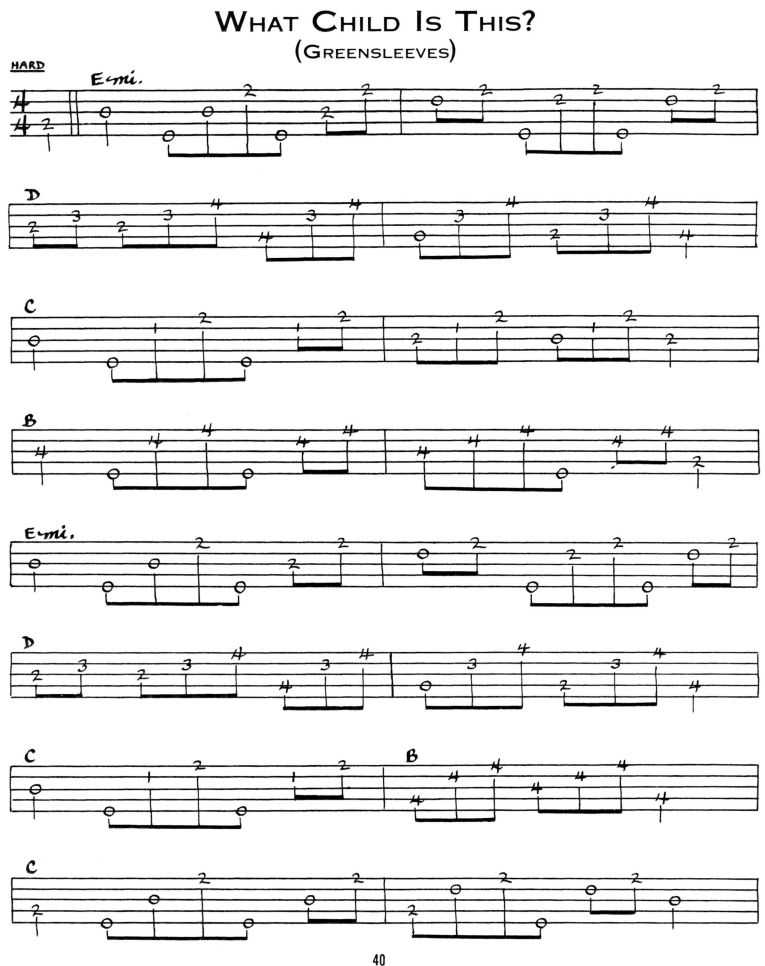

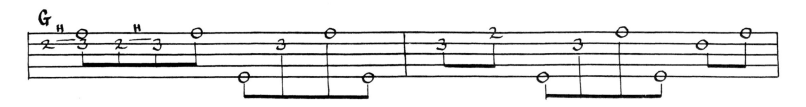

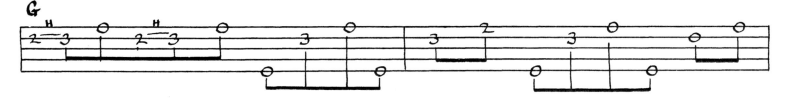

A Christmas Prayer

Let us pray that strength and courage abundant be given
to all who work for a world of reason and understanding ❖
that the good that lies in every man's heart may day by
day be magnified ❖ that men will come to see more clearly
not that which divides them, but that which unites them ❖
that each hour may bring us closer to a final victory, not
of nation over nation, but of man over his own evils and
weaknesses ❖ that the true spirit of this Christmas Season—
its joy, its beauty, its hope, and above all its abiding faith—
may live among us ❖ that the blessings of peace be ours—
the peace to build and grow, to live in harmony and sympa-
thy with others, and to plan for the future with confidence.

More Great Christmas Books from Centerstream...

CHRISTMAS SOUTH OF THE BORDER
featuring the Red Hot Jalapeños
with special guest
The Cactus Brothers
Add heat to your holiday with these ten salsa-flavored arrangements of time-honored Christmas carols. With the accompanying CD, you can play your guitar along with The Cactus Brothers on: Jingle Bells • Deck the Halls • Silent Night • Joy to the World • What Child Is This? • and more. ¡Feliz Navidad!

00000319 Book/CD Pack $19.95

A CLASSICAL CHRISTMAS
by Ron Middlebrook
This book/CD pack features easy to advanced play-along arrangements of 23 top holiday tunes for classical/fingerstyle guitar. Includes: Birthday of a King • God Rest Ye, Merry Gentlemen • Good Christian Men, Rejoice • Jingle Bells • Joy to the World • O Holy Night • O Sanctissima • What Child Is This? (Greensleeves) • and more. The CD features a demo track for each song.

00000271 Book/CD Pack... $15.95

CHRISTMAS UKULELE, HAWAIIAN STYLE
Play your favorite Christmas songs Hawaiian style with expert uke player Chika Nagata. This book/CD pack includes 12 songs, each played 3 times: the first and third time with the melody, the second time without the melody so you can play or sing along with the rhythm-only track. Songs include: Mele Kalikimaka (Merry Christmas to You) • We Wish You a Merry Christmas • Jingle Bells (with Hawaiian lyrics) • Angels We Have Heard on High • Away in a Manger •
Deck the Halls • Hark! The Herald Angels Sing • Joy to the World • O Come, All Ye Faithful • Silent Night • Up on the Housetop • We Three Kings.

00000472 Book/CD Pack $19.95

JAZZ GUITAR CHRISTMAS
by George Ports
Features fun and challenging arrangements of 13 Christmas favorites. Each song is arranged in both easy and intermediate chord melody style. Songs include: All Through the Night • Angels from the Realm of Glory • Away in a Manger • The Boar's Head Carol • The Coventry Carol • Deck the Hall • Jolly Old St. Nicholas • and more.

00000240.. $9.95

CHRISTMAS SOUTH OF THE BORDER
featuring The Cactus Brothers
with Special Guest
Señor Randall Ames
Add heat to your holiday with these Salsa-flavored piano arrangements of time-honored Christmas carols. Play along with the arrangements of Señor Randall Ames on Silent Night, Carol of the Bells, We Three Kings, Away in a Manger, O Come O Come Immanuel, and more. Feliz Navidad!

C0000343 Book/CD Pack $19.95
C0000345 Book/CD Pack $19.95

DOBRO CHRISTMAS
arranged by Stephen F. Toth
Well, it's Christmas time again, and you, your family and friends want to hear some of those favorite Christmas songs on your glistening (like the "trees") Dobro with its bell-like (as in "jingle") tone. This book contains, in tablature format, 2 versions of 20 classic Christmas songs plus a bonus "Auld Lang Syne" for your playing and listening pleasure. The arrangements were created to make them easy to learn, play, remember, or sight read. So get playing and get merry!

00000218.. $9.95

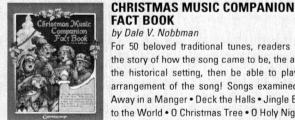

CHRISTMAS MUSIC COMPANION FACT BOOK
by Dale V. Nobbman
For 50 beloved traditional tunes, readers will learn the story of how the song came to be, the author and the historical setting, then be able to play a great arrangement of the song! Songs examined include: Away in a Manger • Deck the Halls • Jingle Bells • Joy to the World • O Christmas Tree • O Holy Night • Silver Bells • We Wish You a Merry Christmas • What Child Is This? • and more!

00000272 112 pages $12.95

THE ULTIMATE CHRISTMAS MUSIC COMPANION FACT BOOK
by Dale Nobbman
This book provides comprehensive biographical sketches of the men and women who wrote, composed, and translated the most famous traditional Christmas songs of all time. Their true-life stories and achievements are fascinating and inspirational for anyone wanting to know more about the people behind the music. 144 pages.

00001178.. $24.95

P.O. Box 17878 - Anaheim Hills, CA 92817
(714) 779-9390   www.centerstream-usa.com

5-STRING BANJO CHORDS
by Ron Middlebrook

The only chart showing the open and moveable chord positions. Explains the two main playing styles, bluegrass and clawhammer, and includes a fingerboard chart.
00000074 ....$2.95

5 STRING BANJO NATURAL STYLE
No Preservatives
by Ron Middlebrook

Now available with a helpful play-along CD, this great songbook for 5-string banjo pickers features 10 easy, 10 intermediate and 10 difficult arrangements of the most popular bluegrass banjo songs. This book/CD pack comes complete with a chord chart.
00000284 Book/CD Pack $17.95

CLASSICAL BANJO [TAB]
40 Classical Works Arranged for the 5-String Banjo
by Kyle R. Datesman

40 works from the Renaissance and Elizabethan period presented in chordal and a more linear manner. Includes an informative introduction about the origins of the music and playing style.
00000179 ....$12.95

BEGINNING CLAWHAMMER BANJO [DVD]
by Ken Perlman

Ken Perlman is one of the most celebrated clawhammer banjo stylists performing today. In this new DVD, he teaches how to play this exciting style, with ample close-ups and clear explanations of techniques such as: hand positions, chords, tunings, brush-thumb, single-string strokes, hammer-ons, pull-offs and slides. Songs include: Boatsman • Cripple Creek • Pretty Polly. Includes a transcription booklet. 60 minutes.
00000330 DVD $19.95

INTERMEDIATE CLAWHAMMER BANJO [DVD]
by Ken Perlman

Picking up where *Beginning Clawhammer Banjo* leaves off, this DVD begins with a review of brush thumbing and the single-string stroke, then moves into specialized techniques such as: drop- and double-thumbing, single-string brush thumb, chords in double "C" tuning, and more. Tunes include: Country Waltz • Green Willis • Little Billie Wilson • Magpie • The Meeting of the Waters • Old Joe Clark • and more! Includes a transcription booklet. 60 minutes.
00000331 DVD $19.95

CLAWHAMMER STYLE BANJO [DVD] [TAB]
A Complete Guide for Beginning and Advanced Banjo Players
by Ken Perlman

This handbook covers basic right & left-hand positions, simple chords, and fundamental clawhammer techniques: the brush, the "bumm-titty" strum, pull-offs, and slides. There is also instruction on more complicated picking, double thumbing, quick slides, fretted pull-offs, harmonics, improvisation, and more. Includes over 40 fun-to-play banjo tunes.
00000118 Book Only.............................$19.95
00000334 DVD $39.95

THE CLASSIC DOUGLAS DILLARD SONGBOOK OF 5-STRING BANJO TABLATURES [TAB]

This long-awaited songbook contains exact transcriptions in banjo tablature that capture the unique playing style of Douglas Dillard. This fantastic collection includes all of his best-loved tunes, from "The Andy Griffith Show" to his solo banjo albums and his releases with The Doug Dillard Band. Features more than 20 tunes in G tuning, C tuning amd G modal tuning, including classics such as: Cripple Creek • Hickory Hollow • Jamboree • John Henry • Old Joe Clark • Buckin' Mule • and more. A must-have for all banjo players!
00000286 ....$19.95

THE EARLY MINSTREL BANJO [TAB]
by Joe Weidlich

Featuring more than 65 classic songs, this interesting book teaches how to play the minstrel banjo like players who were part of various popular troupes in 1865. The book includes: a short history of the banjo, including the origins of the minstrel show; info on the construction of minstrel banjos, chapters on each of the seven major banjo methods published through the end of the Civil War; songs from each method in banjo tablature, many available for the first time; info on how to arrange songs for the minstrel banjo; a reference list of contemporary gut and nylon string gauges approximating historical banjo string tensions in common usage during the antebellum period (for those Civil War re-enactors who wish to achieve that old-time "minstrel banjo" sound); an extensive cross-reference list of minstrel banjo song titles found in the major antebellum banjo methods; and more. (266 pages)
00000325..$29.95

THE BANJO MUSIC OF TONY ELLIS [TAB]

One of Bill Monroe's Bluegrass Boys in the 1960s, Tony Ellis is among the most renowned banjo players around. This superb book assembles songs from four highly acclaimed CDs – Dixie Banner, Farewell My Home, Quaker Girl and Sounds like Bluegrass to Me – capturing his unique two- and three-finger playing techniques in the bluegrass style in standard notation and tab.
00000326 ....$19.95

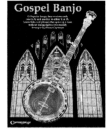

GOSPEL BANJO [TAB]
arranged by Dennis Caplinger

Features 15 spiritual favorites, each arranged in 2 different keys for banjo. Includes: Amazing Grace • Crying Holy • I'll Fly Away • In the Sweet By and By • Just a Closer Walk with Thee • Life's Railway to Heaven • Nearer My God to Thee • Old Time Religion • Swing Low, Sweet Chariot • Wayfaring Stranger • Will the Circle Be Unbroken • more!
00000249 ....$12.95

 **New**

MELODIC CLAWHAMMER BANJO
A Comprehensive Guide to Modern Clawhammer Banjo
by Ken Perlman

Ken Perlman, today's foremost player of the style, brings you this comprehensive guide to the melodic clawhammer. Over 50 tunes in clear tablature. Learn to play authentic versions of Appalachian fiddle tunes, string band tunes, New England hornpipes, Irish jigs, Scottish reels, and more. Includes arrangements by many important contemporary players, and chapters on basic and advanced techniques. Also features over 70 musical illustrations, plus historical notes, and period photos.
00000412 Book/CD Pack $19.95

MINSTREL BANJO – BRIGGS' BANJO INSTRUCTOR [TAB]
by Joseph Weidlich

The Banjo Instructor by Tom Briggs, published in 1855, was the first complete method for banjo. It contained "many choice plantation melodies," "a rare collection of quaint old dances," and the "elementary principles of music." This edition is a reprinting of the original Briggs' *Banjo Instructor*, made up-to-date with modern explanations, tablature, and performance notes. It teaches how to hold the banjo, movements, chords, slurs and more, and includes 68 banjo solo songs that Briggs presumably learned directly from slaves.
00000221 ....$12.95

MORE MINSTREL BANJO [TAB]
by Joseph Weidlich

This is the second book in a 3-part series of intabulations of music for the minstrel (Civil War-era) banjo. Adapted from Frank Converse's *Banjo Instructor, Without a Master* (published in New York in 1865), this book contains a choice collection of banjo solos, jigs, songs, reels, walk arounds, and more, progressively arranged and plainly explained, enabling players to become proficient banjoists. Thorough measure-by-measure explanations are provided for each of the songs, all of which are part of the traditional minstrel repertoire.
00000258 ....$12.95